3 4028 08974 1947

W9-CHV-190

Great Empires

The Aztec Empire

ELLIS ROXBURGH

Cavendish
Square
New York

Published in 2016 by Cavendish Square Publishing, LLC
243 5th Avenue, Suite 136, New York, NY 10016

First Edition

Website: cavendishsq.com

This publication represents the opinions and views of the author based on his or her personal experiences, knowledge, and research. The information in this book serves as a general guide only. the author and publisher have used their best efforts in preparing this book and disclaim liability rising directly or indirectly from the use and application of this book.

CPSIA Compliance Information: Batch #WS15CSQ

Library of Congress Cataloging-in-Publication Data

Roxburgh, Ellis.
The Aztec empire / by Ellis Roxburgh.
p. cm. — (Great Empires)
Includes index.
ISBN 978-1-50260-638-9 (hardcover) ISBN 978-1-50260-639-6 (ebook)
1. Aztecs — Juvenile literature. 2. Aztecs — History — Juvenile literature. 3. Aztecs — Social life
and customs — Juvenile literature.I. Roxburgh, Ellis. II. Title.
F1219.73 R69 2016
972—d23

For Brown Bear Books Ltd:
Editorial Director: Lindsey Lowe
Managing Editor: Tim Cooke
Children's Publisher: Anne O'Daly
Design Manager: Keith Davis
Designer: Melissa Roskell
Picture Manager: Sophie Mortimer

Picture Credits:
Front Cover: British Museum: br; Robert Hunt Library: background.
Alamy: Art Archive 8, 13, Peter M. Wilson 24; British Museum: 4; Getty Images: John Berkley, National Geographic 21;
Robert Hunt Library: 6, 9, 15, 16, 17, 19, 22, 23, 26, 29, 32, 39br; Shutterstock: Julio Aldana 10, Phoo Chan 25, fototehnik 5,
Soft Light 12; Thinkstock: Dorling Kindersley 31, Hemera 34, iStock 11, 14, 27, 33, Photos.com 38/39, 40, 41; TopFoto:
Ann Ronan Picture Library/Heritage Images 35, Granger Collection 30, Roger-Viollet 37, World History Archive 20;
U.S. Library of Congress: 28; Werner Foreman Archive: Museum fur Volkerkunde 42; Windmill Books 1, 7, 15.
Artistic Effects: Shutterstock:

Brown Bear Books has made every attempt to contact the copyright holder.
If you have any information please contact licensing@brownbearbooks.co.uk

Manufactured in the United States of America

CONTENTS

Introduction

In the fourteenth and fifteenth centuries, the Aztecs built an empire that covered much of what is now central Mexico.

The Aztecs are mainly remembered today for two things: their use of human **sacrifice** and the fact that their empire was overthrown by just a handful of Spanish soldiers in 1521. However, the Aztecs were a complex people. After settling in central Mexico, they built an empire through a combination of military strength and forming alliances with their neighbors. They were expert traders, with networks throughout Mexico and Central America. They built a mighty capital at Tenochtitlán.

This double-headed serpent made from wood covered in **turquoise** was probably worn by an Aztec official during religious ceremonies.

The Aztec calendar stone predicted that the Fifth Age of the world, in which the Aztecs lived, would end in the world's destruction.

In the fourteenth century, Mexico was home to a range of peoples. They spoke the same languages and shared similar beliefs, gods, and rituals. The key to the Aztecs' rise to power was the formation in 1428 of the Triple Alliance between Tenochtitlán and its neighbors, Texcoco and Tlacopan. The name Aztec can be used to describe the people of Tenochtitlán but is also used to describe the Triple Alliance. The peoples are sometimes also known as the Mexica—the name gives us the country name, Mexico.

The empire ruled by the Triple Alliance reached its height early in the 16th century. The three central cities ruled conquered peoples who paid taxes to the empire as **tribute**, or donations in the form of goods or labor. It was this tribute that kept the empire wealthy.

At the head of the empire was the emperor in Tenochtitlán. He led a large class of nobles who served as governors of the **provinces** of the empire, as priests, and as warriors. Warfare was at the heart of Aztec life. It was both how the Aztecs conquered more land for the empire and how they captured victims for sacrifice. The Aztecs believed that sacrifice was essential to please the gods who protected them. Myths predicted that the Aztecs' world would end in violence and destruction.

When violence broke out, the lightly armed Aztec warriors were no match for Spanish soldiers using armor and gunpowder.

In 1519, the Aztec emperor Moctezuma II heard that foreigners had landed on the Mexican coast. The newcomers were Spanish soldiers led by Hernán Cortés. They headed toward Tenochtitlán.

Moctezuma made the Spaniards welcome, but other Aztecs soon began to worry that the foreigners were weakening the ruler's power.

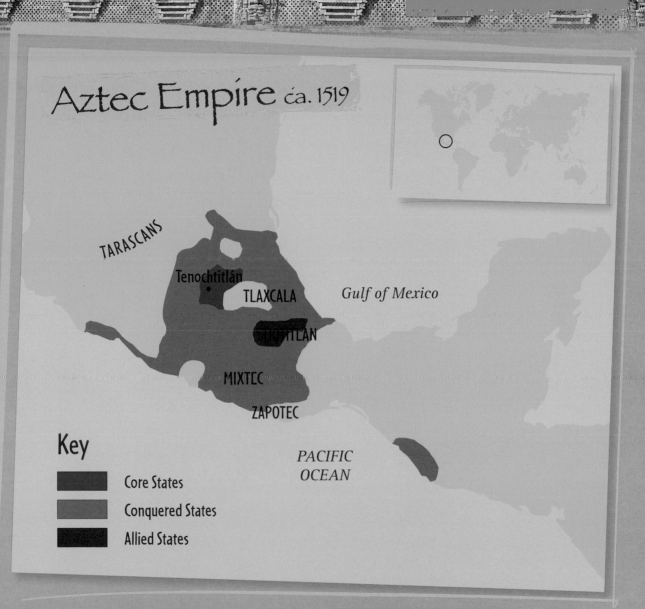

Aztec Empire ca. 1519

TARASCANS

Tenochtitlán

TLAXCALA

Gulf of Mexico

MIXTEC

ZAPOTEC

PACIFIC OCEAN

Key

Core States

Conquered States

Allied States

In June 1520, Aztec warriors drove the Spaniards out of Tenochtitlán. Moctezuma was killed in the fighting. The next year, Cortés gathered his troops and laid siege to the city. On August 13, 1521, the capital surrendered. The Spaniards took charge and began to destroy all signs that the great Aztec Empire had ever existed.

The Roots of the Empire

The origins of the Aztecs are shrouded in mystery. The Aztecs themselves told a story about the founding of their empire that combined legend and history.

According to the story, the Aztecs came from a homeland named Aztlan ("place of the herons" in Nahuatl, the Aztec language). Aztlan was said to be dry and full of cacti. Historians think it may have been in what is now northern Mexico, or the Southwestern United States. The Aztecs lived in Aztlan as hunter-gatherers. They spent most of their time there searching for food.

The Migration Begins

In the early 1100s eight tribes left Aztlan to search for new land. This might have been because they were forced out by their enemies. According to Aztec legend, the tribes—known together as the Chicimec—wandered south.

The god Huitzilpochtli gave the tribes a new name: "Mexica," from which the name Mexico comes. This tribe founded a settlement on Coatepetl (Serpent Mountain), but Huitzilopochtli told

The Aztecs recorded how they eventually found the eagle on top of the prickly cactus that indicated the end of their long journey.

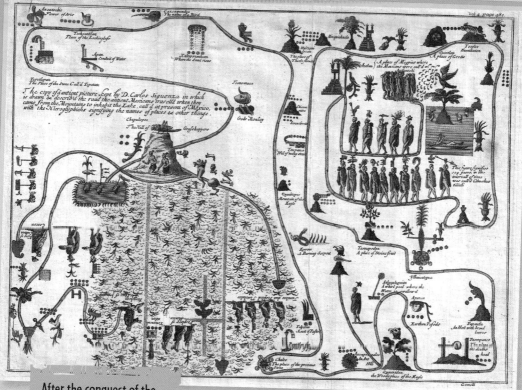

After the conquest of the Aztec Empire in 1521, Spaniards drew maps of the trek based on the stories the Aztec told them.

them to continue wandering. When the female warrior Coyolxauhqui refused, the god's followers killed her. The cult of Huitzilopochtli then became dominant among the Aztecs.

Huitzilopochtli told them that they would be able to identify their new home. They would see an eagle perched on top of a prickly pear cactus, eating a serpent.

BELIEFS

Aztlan

The exact location of the mythical Aztec homeland has fascinated historians for centuries. Many experts suggest that it never actually existed other than as a part of Aztec myth. Others, including the German geographer Alexander von Humboldt (1769–1859), believed it was near the Great Salt Lake in what is now Utah.

Huitzilopochtli

Huitzilopochtli was the most important of the Aztec gods, and not only because he led them from Aztlan to Tenochtitlán. He was also the chief god of war and the god of the sun. He became chief god after the Aztec king Tlacaelel (1397–1487 CE) changed the Aztec religion. Tlacaelel wanted to persuade the Aztecs that they were destined to rise to greatness. This was partly because of their military strength. He told them it was also because Huitzilopochtli favored them.

Huitzilopochtli was the chief war god of the Aztecs. They believed that the fate of the people depended on keeping Huitzilopochtli happy.

The Aztecs moved on. They visited the great ceremonial city of Tula, built by the Toltec. They also visited an abandoned Olmec city with two huge pyramids. The Aztecs named the place Teotihuacan, the "city of the gods."

The Valley of Mexico

After a century of wandering, the Aztecs came to the Valley of Mexico. They were the last of the eight tribes to arrive, and the best land had been taken. The earlier arrivals had established **city-states**, including the Culhua, Acolhua, and the most powerful, the Tepanec.

The Aztecs settled on a rocky hill in Culhua territory named Chapultepec ("grasshopper hill"). The Culhua did not want it because the land was poor.

The Olmec carved huge stone heads that seem to be wearing a type of helmet. The heads may represent Olmec rulers.

which was covered in volcanic rocks and poisonous snakes. Despite this, the Aztecs remained there for the next twenty-five years, learning how to farm in the harsh conditions. Impressed that the Aztecs had succeeded in living on Tizaapan, the Culhua king offered to form an alliance with them. The Aztecs agreed, realizing that an alliance would allow them to create the strongest army in the Valley of Mexico.

The alliance soon ended. The Aztecs sacrificed the daughter of the king of Culhua to Huitzilopochtli. The furious king ordered his warriors to kill the Aztecs. The Aztecs fled to the swamps of Lake Texcoco.

For forty years, the Aztecs grew crops there, but their stay ended when they were attacked by Copil, the son of the sister of Huitzilopochtli. In the battle that followed, the Aztecs killed Copil. It was said that Huitzilopochtli himself cut out Copil's heart and threw it into marshy Lake Texcoco.

The Culhua had grown nervous of the Aztecs and also attacked them. The Aztecs left Chapultepec and settled on Tizaapan,

KEY PEOPLE

The Olmec

The Olmec developed the first complex society in **Mesoamerica** around 1500 BCE. The name "Olmec" was an Aztec word meaning "rubber people," because the Olmec lived where rubber plants grew. The Olmec grew crops, built religious buildings, including **pyramid** temples, and carved stone sculptures. They also sacrificed humans as gifts to their gods. Their culture thrived until 400 BCE.

KEY PEOPLE

Tula

On their journey south, the Aztec visited Tula, the capital of the Toltec. The city had been abandoned nearly two hundred years earlier. The Aztecs described the city as a kind of paradise, where the inhabitants were skilled in sciences and the arts. They told stories about the last ruler of Tula, Quetzalcoatl. In time, they began to worship him as a god.

Lake Texcoco

At the time, Lake Texcoco belonged to the Tepanec. The Tepanec allowed the Aztecs to live on an island in the middle of the swampy marsh. In return, the Aztecs had to pay tribute. Tribute was a kind of taxation paid in goods the Aztecs gave to the Tepanec. The Aztecs also had to supply warriors to fight the Tepanec's enemies.

In the marsh of Texcoco the **prophecy** of Huitzilopochtli finally came true. The Aztecs saw the eagle on top of the cactus, showing the spot where Copil's heart was buried. The Aztecs built a temple to Huitzilopochtli on the site and founded a

The platform at the top of the main pyramid in Tula is topped by 15-foot (4-meter) tall statues of Toltec warriors.

This artist's view shows the Aztecs piling mud on a mat to create a chinampa. More chinampas can be seen in the background.

city around it named Tenochtitlán. The year was 1325 CE. The Aztecs divided their new settlement into four quarters, each built around a ceremonial center with a temple dedicated to Huitzilopochtli.

During the early period of settlement, the Aztecs quarreled among themselves. Some leaders broke away and moved to a nearby island-lagoon, where they built a settlement named Tlatelolco. It would eventually grow to become a powerful rival of Tenochtitlán.

DAILY LIFE

Chinampas

To create land on Lake Texcoco, the Aztecs used a system of chinampas, or floating fields. Farmers created square islands in the canals using willow saplings to anchor in place reed mats covered in mud. The plot of "land" was then ready to plant maize. This unique way of creating land enabled the Aztecs to build their city, Tenochtitlán.

Building the Empire

Tenochtitlán grew into a large city on two islands in the middle of swampy Lake Texcoco. It was a remarkable feat of engineering, and became a mighty capital for the Aztec empire.

The island city had stone temples, plazas, and I-shaped courts for playing a sacred **ball game**. At the heart of the city was the royal complex. On its edges were homes made from **adobe** and farmland constructed with chinampas. Tenochtitlán was connected to the lake shore by a series of raised causeways that made the city easy to defend.

About fifty years after founding the city, the Aztecs chose their first king (*tlatoani*, or "he who speaks"). He was Acamapichtli (ruled circa 1375–1395 CE), and he was a Culhua nobleman. The new king built the Aztecs' power by marrying the daughters of local leaders to earn their loyalty.

The Aztecs were influenced to build stepped pyramids by the Toltec buildings they saw in Tula, and the massive pyramids of Teotihuacan.

Aztec nobles visit the central complex of Tenochtitlán. In the background is the Great Temple, a pyramid with two small shrines on top.

Despite Acamapichtli's strategy, the Aztecs still had to pay tribute to the more powerful Tepanec by giving them goods such as food. Aztec warriors still served in the Tepanec army. In exchange, the Tepanec protected Tenochtitlán and traded with Aztec merchants.

After Acamapichtli's death in 1395, his son Huitzilihuitl became tlatoani. He married the daughter of the Tepanec ruler Tezozomoc (ruled ca. 1367–1426), partly in order to reduce the amount of tribute the Aztecs paid. Huitzilihuitl also helped turn the Aztecs into even better warriors.

Aztec Kings

After Huitzilihuitl's death in 1417, the Tepanec ruler Tezozomoc seized the Aztec throne. On Tezozomoc's death in 1426, his son, Maxtla, killed all his Aztec rivals for

KEY PEOPLE

The Toltec

The Aztecs adopted many ideas from the Toltec of Tula, including human sacrifice and playing a ball game to honor the gods. They also adopted the Toltec god Quetzalcoatl. The Aztecs believed that Quetzalcoatl (whose name means "plumed serpent") was tricked into leaving Toltec land but that one day he would return.

the throne and seized it for himself. The Aztecs were too weak to take on the Tepanec to stop him.

In 1427, the Aztecs chose as tlatoani one of Acamapichtli's sons, Itzcoatl (ruled 1427–1440). Helped by his nephew, Tlacaelel, Itzcoatl formed alliances against Maxtla and the Tepanec. Itzcoatl formed the Triple Alliance in 1428 with Texcoco and Tlacopan against the Tepanec.

The Tepanec army had a fearsome reputation, but the Aztecs and their allies attacked them head on, rather than surrounding them, as was a more common military tactic at the time. The Tepanec fled, and the Aztecs destroyed the Tepanec city of Azcapotzalco to ruins. This was also unusual at the time.

DAILY LIFE

Tribute

Tribute was a form of taxation that city-states paid to more powerful states. States paid tribute to the Triple Alliance in return for retaining their own rulers. Tribute often took the form of goods, such as wood or cacao beans. Tribute could also be paid in the form of work. The amount of tribute varied from state to state but was paid once or twice a year. Virtually everyone paid taxes or tribute throughout the empire.

Acamapichtli developed the strategy of building alliances that began the Aztecs rise to power in the region.

Victory of the Triple Alliance

The Triple Alliance divided Tepanec territory, but although the Tepanec were weakened they were not destroyed. A city named Coyocan resisted until Aztec warriors destroyed it and finally defeated the last Tepanec warriors in battle.

The Triple Alliance was now in firm control of the Valley of Mexico. It set about building its power. It conquered city-states in what are now central and southern Mexico. It divided its new territory into provinces. The provinces had to pay tribute to the Triple Alliance. This helped keep them under control

DAILY LIFE

The Flower Wars

The Flower Wars were battles the Aztecs fought with their neighbors so that both sides could take prisoners. Victory or defeat were not very important. The battles were a means of training warriors and ensuring a supply of captives to be used for human sacrifice. The battles only took place when it was convenient for both sides.

An Aztec Jaguar Warrior in full costume (right) prepares to fight an opponent from a neighboring tribe during one of the Flower Wars.

The Height of the Empire

In 1440, Huitzilihuitl's son, Moctezuma, became the new tlatoani. The new ruler planned to expand the empire to stretch from the Pacific Ocean in the west to the Gulf of Mexico in the east.

The empire had become rich thanks to tribute from the conquered tribes. Moctezuma (ruled 1440–1469) used this wealth to improve Tenochtitlán with new temples, homes, and roads. He made sure that his warriors were richly rewarded and that his people were fed and had work.

He also built alliances with tribes conquered by his predecessors. He believed that the way to achieve his expansion plan was to keep the gods happy. He sent wise men north to find Aztlan, the place where legend said their ancestors had originated. The wise men

This illustration from after the Spanish conquest shows Aztec warriors defending the Great Temple in the heart of Tenochtitlán.

The Jaguar Warriors were among the most feared Aztec warriors. They carried clubs with blades made from sharp, glasslike obsidian.

retraced the ancient journey. On the way, they heard a prophecy that Huitzilopochtli and the Aztecs would lose their power.

Prophecies of Disaster

Moctezuma was unhappy to hear about the prophecy. Everything seemed to be going well. However, soon afterward, several natural disasters seemed to be bad **omens**. A plague of locusts descended on the Valley of Mexico. They ate all the crops, so the Aztecs had to eat the grain they had stored in the royal granaries. Moctezuma ordered human sacrifices to keep the gods happy. Then, in 1449, Tenochtitlán flooded as heavy rains caused the waters of Lake Texcoco to rise. The next year, a frost that killed the crops was followed by a drought.

KEY PEOPLE

Tlacaelel

Tlacaelel (1397–1487) was an outstanding Aztec leader. He created the myth that the Aztecs were a chosen race. He said Huitzilopochtli had promised to make the Aztecs great, if they offered him human sacrifices. Realizing that conquest was the best way to acquire sacrificial victims, he improved Aztec military power by inventing the Flower Wars so that warriors could practice their skills.

The New Fire Ceremony

In 1454, the two Aztec calendars—the 260-day sacred calendar and the 360-day seasonal calendar—started on the same day. This only happened every fifty-two years. After a five-day cleansing period, all fires in the empire were put out. A new fire was lit in the Great Temple, from which fires in smaller temples, palaces, and homes were lit and a new fifty-two-year cycle began.

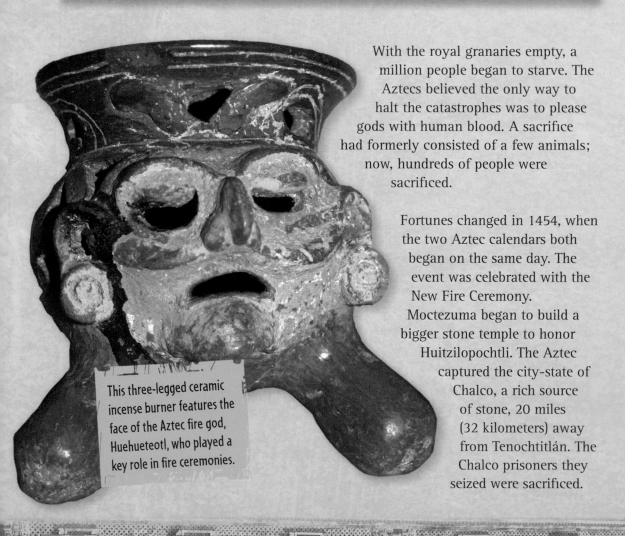

This three-legged ceramic incense burner features the face of the Aztec fire god, Huehueteotl, who played a key role in fire ceremonies.

With the royal granaries empty, a million people began to starve. The Aztecs believed the only way to halt the catastrophes was to please gods with human blood. A sacrifice had formerly consisted of a few animals; now, hundreds of people were sacrificed.

Fortunes changed in 1454, when the two Aztec calendars both began on the same day. The event was celebrated with the New Fire Ceremony. Moctezuma began to build a bigger stone temple to honor Huitzilopochtli. The Aztec captured the city-state of Chalco, a rich source of stone, 20 miles (32 kilometers) away from Tenochtitlán. The Chalco prisoners they seized were sacrificed.

Tenochtitlán was joined to the shores of Lake Texcoco by causeways that also carried fresh water to the city.

After Moctezuma died in 1468, the Aztec elders wanted his advisor, Tlacaelel, to become the new king. Tlacaelel refused, preferring to be the power behind the throne for Moctezuma's young son, Axayacatl (ruled 1469–1481).

Axayacatl set out to expand the empire. After his army put down a rebellion in the neighboring city of Tlatelolco, Axayacatl turned to the Tarascans, the Aztecs' main rivals in the west. In 1478, the Tarascans easily defeated the Aztec at Tzintzuntzan, the main Tarascan city. Of the forty thousand Aztec warriors who set out, only two thousand returned to Tenochtitlán.

Despite this heavy defeat, Axayacatl's position was strengthened when the king of Texcoco, Nezahualcoyotl, died in 1472

DAILY LIFE

Fresh Water

Aqueducts carried fresh water to Tenochtitlan from up to 7.5 miles (12 km) away. The engineer who designed them was most likely Nezahualcoyotl, the ruler of Texcoco. The **aqueduct** was made from mud, so it eroded over time. Moctezuma II later built a double aqueduct to bring more fresh water into the city.

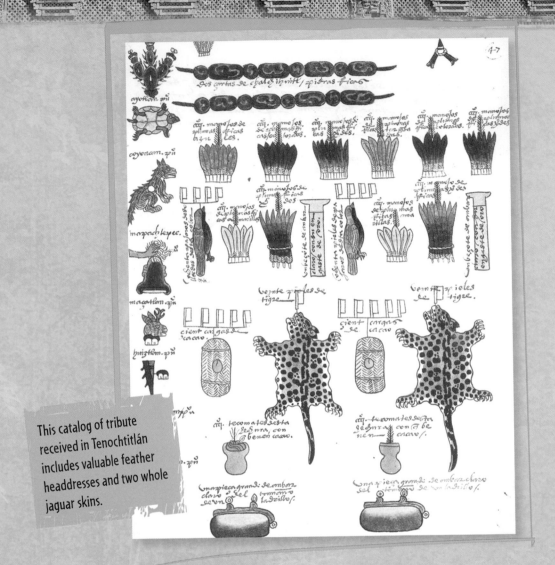

This catalog of tribute received in Tenochtitlán includes valuable feather headdresses and two whole jaguar skins.

without an heir. Because Texcoco was a member of the Triple Alliance, Axayacatl was able to claim the empty throne, increasing Aztec power. When Axayactl died in 1481, his brother Tizoc took over. He was a weak king whose short rule achieved very little. There was great relief when his brother, Ahuitzotl, came to the throne in 1486.

The Height of Aztec Power

A fine military strategist, Ahuitzotl finally took control of areas that had resisted Aztec domination to the south and west of Tenochtitlán in 1491 and 1495. The newly defeated regions paid tribute that included cacao beans used to make chocolate, which the Aztecs highly prized. By 1495, the empire of the Triple Alliance was so large it was becoming increasingly hard to manage. In Tenochtitlan, Texcoco, and Tlacopan, rulers wanted ever more magnificent temples and palaces and fine clothes and jewelry. The burden of tribute on the subjugated peoples grew.

When Moctezuma II became tlatoani in 1502 (ruled 1502–1520), the empire was at breaking point. Moctezuma had firm ideas about the empire. Life in the Triple Alliance seemed to be stable—but its stability was about to be tested.

DAILY LIFE

Tlatelolco

Tlatelolco was Tenochtitlan's sister city and market; they were probably founded around the same time. Initially, the two cities cooperated to defeat common enemies such as the Tepanec, but this changed under Axayacatl (1469-1481). Tlatelolco rebelled against paying tribute to Tenochtitlán. Axayacatl stopped the rebellion and Tenochtitlán took control of the city.

The Great Temple of Tenochtitlán rises in the background of this 3-D clay model of the busy marketplace in Tlatelolco.

The Peoples of the Empire

The empire of the Triple Alliance was built on military conquest and the defeat of other city-states, whose peoples were forced to join the growing empire.

The Triple Alliance of the Tlacopan, Aztecs, and Texcoco began as a defensive alliance against military attack by the Tepanec. As the empire grew dependent on tribute from defeated enemies, however, it tried to win more victories to ensure it received more tribute. The wealthier the empire grew, the more wealth it wanted.

By 1502, the empire was so big it was divided into districts. Each district had its own schedule of tribute payments. The tribute goods varied from quetzal feathers to stone. They were traded in Tenochtitlán's markets or sent to the royal palaces. Resentment of the tribute system led many of the Aztecs' neighbors to cooperate with the Spaniards when the European invaders arrived in 1519.

The Pyramid of the Niches stands at El Tajín, in southern Mexico. The city was likely part of Totonac territory during the Aztec period.

The quetzal of the Central American forests has long green and red feathers. The feathers were used to make luxury clothing.

Different Aztec rulers fought different enemies. Itzcoatl conquered most of the empire of the Tepanec who had once controlled the Aztecs and forced them to pay tribute. Itzcoatl defeated the Tepanec in battle in 1428.

The Tarascans

The Tarascans were the Aztecs' main rivals in the west, where they lived around Lake Patzcuaro. Like the Aztecs, they were a warring people who expanded their territory by conquering their neighbors. They controlled areas that produced goods the Aztecs valued, such as honey, feathers, cotton, salt, gold, and copper.

Quetzal Feathers

The quetzal that lives in the forests of Mesoamerica has bright green and red plumage. Its feathers were so highly prized by the Aztec that only the emperor and priests were allowed to wear them. The bird was considered sacred, and it was a crime punishable by death to kill one. The feathers were plucked from the tails of living birds. The quetzal lives in remote rain forests, so the Aztec tried to conquer those regions to ensure a ready supply of feathers.

This glyph, or symbol, represents the cities of the Triple Alliance: (from left) Texcoco, Tenochtitlán, and Tlacopan.

Luxury Trade

The Aztecs believed that luxuries were an important sign of someone's rank in society. For that reason, they put great effort into acquiring precious stones, metals, feathers, and even foods such as cacao. Such things were only permitted to be owned or used by a very small ruling **elite**. In that way, rulers, priests, and other leaders showed in their clothes and their lifestyle how rich and powerful they were.

Axayacatl wanted to gain access to these resources. He sent ambassadors to tell the Tarascans to accept Aztec rule, but the Tarascans ignored them. Their well-trained warriors carried better weapons than the Aztecs—they were copper, rather than stone like Aztec weapons. In the battle that followed, the Aztecs were defeated. The Tarascan Empire survived until the arrival of the Spaniards in 1519.

Totonac Resistance

The Totonac lived in eastern Mexico. Although the Aztecs made a series of attempts to conquer them, they were not able to bring them completely under control. Rebellions against the Triple Alliance broke out regularly, and the Totonac would play a large part in the downfall of the Aztecs by siding with the Spanish explorer Hernán Cortés in 1519.

Helping Cortés

The Tlaxcala also helped Cortés. Living in central Mexico east of the Popocétcpetl Volcano, the Tlaxcala constantly warred with the Aztecs but were never conquered. When the Spaniards arrived the Tlaxcala, eager for revenge on the Aztecs, allied themselves with the Europeans. They supplied most of the men who fought under the Spanish flag against the Aztecs. In return, the Tlaxcala were granted special status by the Spaniards in the new colony and paid no tribute to the European rulers, unlike most of the other native peoples.

Moving Around

As the Aztec empire grew, it was important for its rulers and administrators to keep in touch with distant parts of it. Wheeled vehicles did not exist, and the Aztec did not use animals for transport. Instead, they built a road network along which warriors and traders walked, and tribute was carried to Tenochtitlán. There were rest stops every 6 to 9 miles (10 to 15 km) where people could eat or sleep. Within Tenochtitlán itself, so many people moved around the city in canoes that the canals were sometimes completely overcrowded with small craft.

The Pyramid of Flowers dominated the city of Xochitecatl, which was once the ruling city of the region of Tlaxcala.

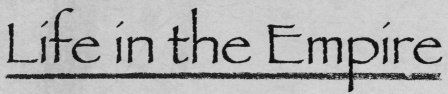

Life in the Empire

Aztec life was highly organized. Everyone in the empire had a specific task, even the emperor. The state protected and fed the people, and shaped all aspects of their lives.

The Aztecs had a rigid social structure, with three classes: nobles, commoners, and slaves. People were born into their class and had little opportunity to move out of it. At the head of the nobility (pipiltin) was the king, or tlatoani, the undisputed head of the empire. To gain closer access to the emperor, other nobles had to marry well, serve the empire, or enjoy military success. Noble status was hereditary, but although nobles enjoyed a privileged position—they ate better food, and lived in more substantial and comfortable houses—they were still expected to work. Many worked as government officials, judges, or military leaders. Noble women worked in the home.

An Aztec priest holds up a beating heart he has just cut from a victim's chest during a sacrifice to the war god Huitzilopochtli.

Aztec Priests

After the tlatoani, the most powerful men in Aztec society were the priests. They kept the gods happy and told the people what the gods needed. High priests were nobles, but others came from other classes. Unmarried women could also become priestesses. The most powerful priests served in the Great Temple. Priests worked in the temple: Some performed sacrifices while others taught religious studies or even served in the army.

Each city-state in the empire had its own tlatoani, who as well as being king was also the commander-in-chief of the army and the high priest. He came from the Aztec royal family, which was very large because each king was allowed to have up to one hundred wives. The most important tlatoani was the ruler of Tenochtitlán. All the others had to obey him. Once elected, a tlatoani served for life.

Warfare and Warriors

War was at the heart of Aztec life. It was the means by which the empire expanded, and it was also the most important way of acquiring the large number of victims needed for human sacrifice. Training to be a warrior started in boyhood. By the age

This stone figure represents the goddess Chicomecoatl, who was one of the chief dieties of corn, the most important Aztec food.

of seventeen, every healthy male was trained to use weapons and was expected to fight if called upon.

Warriors earned the respect of the Aztec people, and their special status was reflected in the uniforms they wore. The greater the military ability of a warrior, the more spectacular his uniform. The two most respected groups of warriors were

Priests hold down a victim while another offers his heart to Huitzilopochtli, this time in his role as the sun god.

the jaguar knights and the eagle knights, who wore special helmets and carried special shields that depicted their animal.

An Aztec warrior had several kinds of weapon. They included spears, slings, bows and arrows, spear-throwers, knives, and swords. The blades were made from obsidian, a type of hard, glasslike stone.

The army was divided into small groups of about two hundred men who combined into larger battalions up to eight thousand men. Some two hundred thousand warriors would take part in a major military campaign.

Gods and Sacrifice

Aztec life was structured around the worship of hundreds of gods and goddesses. The Aztecs inherited many of these from cultures they had conquered, such as the

The Great Temple (above, right) was part of a sacred precinct that contained other temples and a ritual ball court.

Toltec god Quetzalcoatl. The Aztecs believed the gods were involved in every aspect of daily life. When bad things happened, they believed the gods were punishing them. They also thought that hostile natural phenomena such as lightning or drought were caused when the gods were angry.

The Aztec Gods

Huitzilopochtli, the chief god of war and the sun, who had also led the Aztecs to Mexico from Aztlan, was one of the three major Aztec gods. Tezcatlipoca was another war god, but was also associated with the night sky, kingship, and magic.

BELIEFS

The Great Temple

At the heart of the empire was the Great Temple in Tenochtitlán. The pyramid towered over the city and contained two shrines. Huitzilopochtli's shrine was painted blood red. The other temple, painted blue, was dedicated to Tlaloc, the rain god. The Great Temple stood on the site of what is now the main square of Mexico City.

The Nahuatl Language

The Aztec and many of the other peoples of the Valley of Mexico spoke Nahuatl. Because it was the language of the dominant Triple Alliance, Nahuatl was the best language for people to learn and use. It was written down in a series of glyphs—picture symbols—in codices and other records during the height of the Aztec Empire. Today, more than one million people across Mexico still speak Nahuatl.

Coatlicue was the mother of Huitzilopochtli and of the moon and stars. In Nahuatl, her name means "She with the Skirt of Serpents."

The third god, Quetzalcoatl, was god of civilization, priests, and learning. Aztec myths told stories about the rivalry between Tezcatlipoca and Quetzalcoatl. It was said that Tezcatlipoca had tricked Quetzalcoatl when he was ruler of Tula and forced him to leave the Toltec city.

Food and Drink

The staples of the Aztecs were foods that are still eaten today: corn, beans, squash, avocados, tomatoes, and peppers. The staple dish was the tortilla made from corn (maize). Girls learned at an early age how to prepare tortillas. Only wealthier nobles could afford to eat meat. Dogs and turkeys were raised for meat and hunters killed deer, rabbit, ducks, and geese. There were no sheep, pigs, or cattle, until they were introduced by the Spaniards in the 1500s. Popular treats for the tlatoani and other nobles were roasted worms and grasshoppers.

Octli was a popular drink made from the agave plant. The agave sap was boiled and fermented until it turned into a smooth alcoholic drink. Strict rules were meant to stop people drinking too much octli, but these rules were often ignored. Only the richest households could afford to drink hot chocolate made from cacao beans,

DAILY LIFE

Importance of Corn

Indian corn (maize) was the staple food, and the Aztecs used it in a variety of ways. It was ground into flour to make tortillas and tamales, which were eaten at nearly every meal. The kernels were eaten as an early type of popcorn. Corn was also used to make drinks. Growing corn was a key reason why the peoples of Mexico settled in communities, instead of hunting and gathering food as they had done in Aztlan.

Different varieties of corn were grown widely in Central and South America. The food was a staple diet for many powerful cultures.

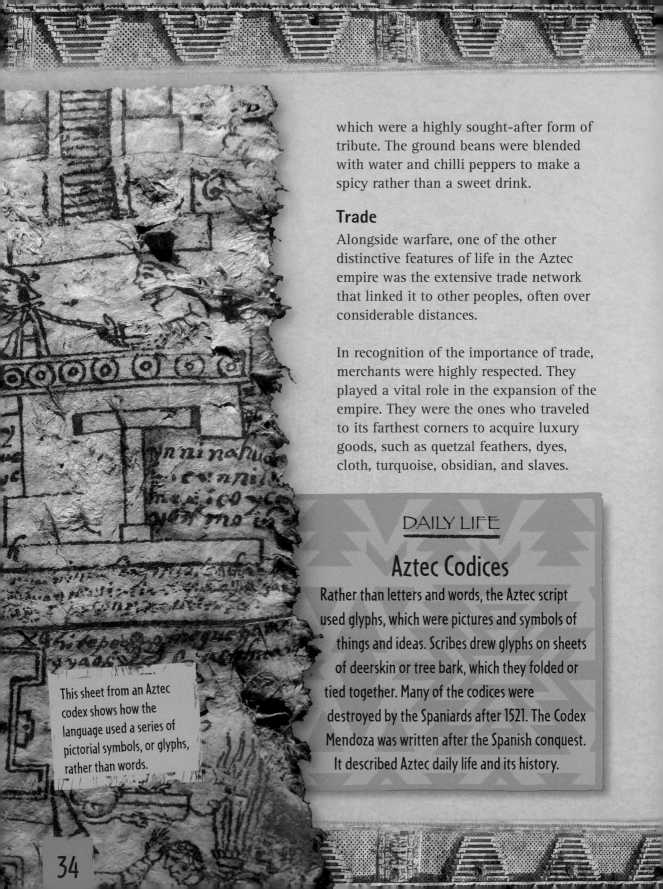

which were a highly sought-after form of tribute. The ground beans were blended with water and chilli peppers to make a spicy rather than a sweet drink.

Trade

Alongside warfare, one of the other distinctive features of life in the Aztec empire was the extensive trade network that linked it to other peoples, often over considerable distances.

In recognition of the importance of trade, merchants were highly respected. They played a vital role in the expansion of the empire. They were the ones who traveled to its farthest corners to acquire luxury goods, such as quetzal feathers, dyes, cloth, turquoise, obsidian, and slaves.

This sheet from an Aztec codex shows how the language used a series of pictorial symbols, or glyphs, rather than words.

DAILY LIFE

Aztec Codices

Rather than letters and words, the Aztec script used glyphs, which were pictures and symbols of things and ideas. Scribes drew glyphs on sheets of deerskin or tree bark, which they folded or tied together. Many of the codices were destroyed by the Spaniards after 1521. The Codex Mendoza was written after the Spanish conquest. It described Aztec daily life and its history.

DAILY LIFE

Education

Both boys and girls went to school. Boys learned trade skills, citizenship, and military training. Girls learned to sing and dance. The children of nobles learned their social obligations and Aztec history. Few Aztec learned how to read and write. The job of a scribe (*tlaacuilo*) was highly respected.

The most valuable goods went straight into the treasuries of the king. The merchants also acted as spies known as *pochteca*, gathering information about the peoples of the empire.

Jewelry and Clothing

As the empire expanded, the tlatoani grew used to the magnificent goods that were constantly brought back to Tenochtitlán. Gold and silver were used to make fine jewelry for the nobility. The brilliant green feathers of the quetzal bird were only permitted to be worn by the tlatoani and the highest-ranking nobles. There were strict rules about what color of clothing a person could wear, depending on his or her position in society: only the tlatoani could wear teal or turquoise, while priests wore black or dark green.

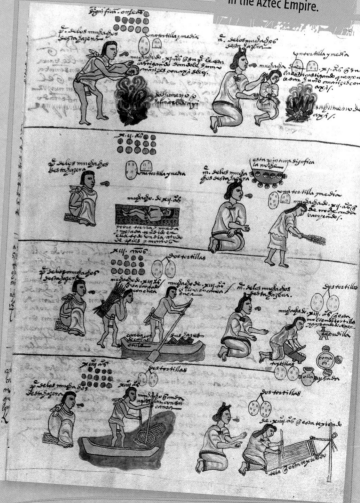

This codex page shows scenes from everyday life in the Aztec Empire.

Fall of the Empire

In February 1519, the Spaniard Hernán Cortés landed with five hundred men on the island of Cozumel off the Yucatan Peninsula. In just over two years, he destroyed the mighty Aztec Empire.

Hernán Cortés (left) meets Moctezuma II. To begin with, the Aztec ruler treated the Spaniards with great respect.

At home in Spain, Cortés (1485–1547) heard the rumors about the riches of the New World and wanted to see them for himself. He sailed to Cuba, where the governor, Diego Velásquez, forbade him to go to Mexico. Cortés sailed for Mexico anyway. On Cozumel, Cortés soon learned of a Spaniard who lived nearby. Gerónimo de Aguilar had been shipwrecked eight years earlier. Cortés hired Aguilar as a translator. This was because Aguilar spoke Mayan. Cortés also used a local slave, Doña Marina (ca. 1501–1550), as a translator, because she spoke both Mayan and Nahuatl.

In Tenochtitlán, Emperor Moctezuma II soon learned of the arrival of the bearded white men. He sent a delegation to meet them with gifts of turquoise, feathers, and gold. The Spaniards

guzmā. michvacā.

This drawing from a codex shows Spaniards on horseback fighting with their native allies against Native American warriors.

showed little interest in the semiprecious stones or feathers but were impressed by the gold. Cortés put on a show for the Aztecs. In full armor and on horseback, the Spaniards waved their swords as Cortés fired his cannon. The Aztecs were terrified because they had never seen either horses or gunpowder. They were also confused because it did not appear that the Spaniards wanted to be friendly.

Greeting Moctezuma

When Moctezuma heard about this first meeting with the Spaniards, he sent another group to meet them. These warriors and priests took with them captives to sacrifice when they arrived. This horrified the Spaniards.

KEY PEOPLE

Hernán Cortés

Hernán Cortés grew up in poverty wanting to be a soldier. He left Spain aged eighteen for Hispaniola and Cuba. Hearing that Mexico was rich in gold, Cortés sailed there in 1519. After the fall of the Aztec, Cortés became governor of New Spain in 1523. He was so dominant that the Spanish king had to limit his powers. Cortés moved back to Spain in 1541, a bitter man.

The Spaniards' gunpowder weapons gave them an advantage even when fighting far larger armies of Alliance opponents.

KEY PEOPLE

Disobeying Orders

In Cuba, Cortés was clerk to the governor, Diego Vélazquez. When the Spaniards heard of Mexico's supplies of gold, Vélazquez asked Cortés to lead an expedition there. But the governor grew jealous and tried to cancel the trip. Cortés ignored him and set sail.

Cortés had learned from the Totonac—enemies of the Aztecs—about Tenochtitlán and its fabulous wealth. He was eager to see it for himself. When some of his men wanted to return to Cuba—Cortés had, after all, disobeyed Governor Velásquez—Cortés burned his own ships. His men had no choice. They started the 200-mile (320 km) march inland to Tenochtitlán.

On the way, the Spaniards defeated the Otomi and the Potoncháns, and made an alliance with the Tlaxcala. The Tlaxcala then tricked their enemies, the Cholula,

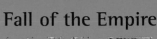

into believing they and the Spaniards came in peace. With their guard down, they were easily defeated. When the Aztecs heard about the defeat of the Cholula, they assumed the Spaniards must have a powerful army.

The Spaniards arrived in Tenochtitlán, where Moctezuma showered them with gifts, including more gold. He intended the gifts to show how powerful the Aztec Empire was. The Spaniards did not understand the message, however. Seeing the gold, they became greedy for more.

La Malinche stands at Cortés's side. She acted as an interpreter during his negotiations with the Aztec peoples.

Like other Europeans, they prized gold for its monetary value: but the Aztecs appreciated it more for its capacity to be made into beautiful objects.

An Astonishing City

When the Spaniards reached Tenochtitlán, they were astonished. Compared with towns in Spain, it was advanced and clean. However, despite the sophistication of the city, the Europeans saw human sacrifice as a sign that the Aztecs were barbarians.

Moctezuma II invited Cortés and his men to stay in his palace. The Spaniards gradually turned him into a **puppet ruler** by influencing all his decisions. They took all the gold he had in his palace. Seeing that the king's powers were being undermined, the Aztec **elders deposed** Moctezuma II and appointed his brother, Cuitlahuac (ruled 1520), in his place.

At this time, Cortés was in an uncomfortable position. Governor Velásquez had sent men to arrest him for disobeying orders. Leaving Pedro de Alvarado (ca. 1485–1541) in charge of Tenochtitlán, Cortés set out to turn back Velásquez's men. While he was gone, Alvarado ordered his men to attack the Aztec. It was a dreadful mistake. The Aztecs fought back and when Cortés returned to Tenochtitlán, he realized that

After the overthrow of the Aztecs, Spanish conquistadors throw the bodies of Moctezuma and a noble into a canal.

the Spanish had to leave the city to avoid being attacked. As they tried to slip away at night on July 1, 1520, the Aztecs stopped them. In the clash that followed, two-thirds of the Spaniards were killed along with one thousand Tlaxcala warriors.

The Final Battle

For now, the Aztecs were victorious, but having glimpsed the wealth of the empire, Cortés would not give it up easily. He waited for Spanish reinforcements to arrive from Cuba. Just as the Aztecs started to believe the threat from the Spaniards had disappeared, another terrible blow hit them. In September 1520, smallpox killed thousands of Aztecs. The Spaniards had unknowingly brought the germs that caused the disease with them. With no immunity to it, the Aztecs had

A Hidden City

Much of Tenochtitlán was destroyed during the eighty-day siege by the Spaniards. The conquerors set fire to buildings, pulled down temples, and destroyed statues. They reused stones to build their own structures on top of Aztec buildings. The main square of Mexico City–the Zócalo–was built directly over the Great Temple. During construction work in recent decades, more and more of the Aztec city has been revealed.

This wall carved with skulls was once part of the Great Temple. It was uncovered during construction work in Mexico City.

The Myth of Quetzalcoatl

One explanation for how a small group of Europeans overthrew a huge empire is the myth of Quetzalcoatl. According to Aztec legend, the feather-serpent god ruled the Toltec before the god of evil, Tezcatlipoca, tricked him into leaving. Quetzalcoatl promised to return one day, which the Aztecs predicted would be in 1519. When Cortés appeared in 1519, some Aztecs may have believed the god had returned to save the people.

Some people believe the myth of Quetzalcoatl's return played a large role in the fall of the Aztecs; others argue that it did not.

no resistance. Cuitlahuac died as well, possibly as one of the disease's victims. Cortés continued to plan his revenge on the Aztecs.

In December 1520, Cortés and his allies marched on the Aztecs' capital. There, they built ships to use to **besiege** the city. On May 30, 1521, the Spaniards launched the ships on Lake Texcoco. They prevented the Aztecs from transporting supplies. The siege lasted for eighty days. During this time, Cortés and his men gradually fought their

The calendar stone recorded the Aztec ritual calendar that saw history as a series of five ages, each of which ended in a great disaster.

way to the center of Tenochtitlán. They captured the last tlatoani, Cuauhtemoc, and by August 13, 1521, Tenochtitlán had fallen to the Spaniards.

Spanish Empire

The Spaniards took over the empire. They allowed the Aztecs to choose their own leaders, but Spaniards were in charge. They pulled down the temples and set about converting the Aztecs to Catholicism. The gold Cortés wanted so badly was sent back to Spain. It would be three hundred years before the descendants of the Aztecs got rid of their colonial rulers.

The Aztec Today

There are about 1.5 million modern Mexicans who claim to be descended from the Aztecs. These Nahua live in communities scattered across the Mexican countryside. They still speak the Nahuatl language, and although many have adopted Christian beliefs, they also preserve traditional practices, such as making offerings to the old gods, including the blood of sacrificed chickens.

Timeline

Sixth century	The first Nahuatl-speaking peoples arrive in central Mexico.
ca. 1100	The Mexica, or Aztecs, leave their mythical homeland of Aztlan and begin over a century of wandering in search of a new place to settle.
1248	The Aztecs settle near Lake Texcoco but are soon expelled by the powerful Tepanec people.
1299	The Aztecs settle on Culhuacan territory at Tizapan.
1325	After a violent disagreement with the Culhuaca, the Aztecs found Tenochtitlán in the swamps of Lake Texcoco.
ca. 1350	The Aztecs dig canals to drain their city, which is supported on submerged foundations in the swamps. Causeways link the city to the shores of Lake Texcoco.
1376	Acamapichitli becomes the first Aztec tlatoani, or emperor.
1390	Construction begins on the Great Temple, a sacred area in the middle of Tenochtitlán.
1395	Huitzilihuitzli comes to the throne in Tenochtitlán. He creates an alliance with the Tepanec.
1417	Chimalpopoca becomes emperor.
1427	Itzcoatl comes to the throne after the assassination of Chimalpopoca by the Tepanec. He goes to war against the Tepanec.

1431	After defeating the Tepanec, Itzcoatl forms the Triple Alliance, with the Tepanec of Tlacopan and the Acolhua who live in Texcoco.
1440	Moctezuma I becomes the fifth Aztec emperor.
1452	Tenochtitlán suffers from severe flooding, followed by three years of famine.
1469	Azayactl comes to the throne.
1481	Tizoc becomes emperor.
1486	Ahuitzotl becomes emperor. The following year, he oversees the reconstruction of the Great Temple.
1502	The ninth emperor comes to the Aztec throne: Moctezuma II.
1519	Spaniards led by Hernán Cortés land on the Yucatan peninsula on March 4. On November 8, they arrive in Tenochtitlán, where they are welcomed by Moctezuma.
1520	After Aztec elders replace Moctezuma with Cuitahuac, the Spaniards and their allies, the Tlaxcala, are driven out of Tenochtitlán overnight on July 1, with heavy losses. Cuitahauac dies, probably in a smallpox epidemic, and is replaced by the last emperor, Cuauhetemoc.
1521	The Spaniards besiege Tenochtitlán. They cut off its supplies and fight their way to the center, where Cuauhetemoc surrenders on August 13. The Spaniards destroy the city.
1522	Mexico city is built on top of the ruins of Tenochtitlán as the capital of the new Spanish Empire.

Glossary

adobe A kind of sun-dried clay used as a building material.

aqueduct A pipe or channel that carries water from a source to the place where it will be used.

ball game A ritual game throughout Mesoamerica in which teams competed to pass a ball through a hoop using their hips and legs.

besiege To surround a city or other location in order to force it to surrender.

city-state An independent state that includes a city and its surrounding territory.

depose To remove someone from office suddenly or by force.

elders The senior figures of a tribe or other group.

elite A small, powerful group of the most influential people in a society.

Mesoamerica A region stretching from southern Mexico to Honduras and Nicaragua, where numerous societies flourished before Europeans arrived in the Americas.

omen An event that is interpreted as a sign that something good or bad will happen.

prophecy A prediction of something that will happen in the future.

province A region of a country or empire that is run as a unit.

puppet ruler A ruler whose power depends on someone else, and who carries out their will.

pyramid A four-sided building that tapers toward the top with smooth sides or in a series of steps.

sacrifice Killing an animal or a human as a gift to the gods, or offering possessions to the gods.

tribute Payment made by one state to another on which it is dependent; tribute often took the form of goods or labor.

turquoise A gemstone colored greenish blue that is often used to make jewelry.

Further Reading

Books

Apte, Sunita. *The Aztec Empire.* True Books. New York: Children's Press, 2010.

Bingham, Jame. *The Aztec Empire.* Time Travel Guides. Chicago: Raintree, 2007.

Deary, Terry. *The Angry Aztecs.* Horrible Histories. London, England: Scholastic, 2008.

Doeden, Matt. *The Aztecs: Life in Tenochtitlán.* Life in Ancient Civilizations. Minneapolis, MN: Millbrook Press, 2009.

Guillain, Charlotte. *Aztec Warriors.* Fierce Fighters. Chicago: Raintree, 2010.

Websites

The History Channel
www.history.com/topics/aztecs
Stories and videos from The History Channel about Aztec civilization.

Kids Info
www.kidinfo.com/
american_history/ancient_americas_
culture.htm
The Kids Info site has links to information about the Aztec as well as other Mesoamerican civilizations.

Mr Donn
www.aztecs.mrdonn.org
Information about daily life in Tenochtitlán, the chinampas, Aztec inventions, and more.

Publisher's note to educators and parents: Our editors have carefully reviewed these websites to ensure that they are suitable for students. Many websites change frequently, however, and we cannot guarantee that a site's future contents will continue to meet our high standards of quality and educational value. Be advised that students should be closely supervised whenever they access the Internet.

Index